Resting Merry
Discovering Joy & Peace at Christmas

DUANE S. MONTAGUE

DEDICATION

This book is dedicated to my family.
Without them, I would not truly know how to Rest Merry.
Thanks for putting up with my Christmas obsession.

Robyn
Audrey
Austen
Autumn
August

Merry Christmas. Bless us all!

INTRODUCTION

It's the season of familiar, wonderful, beautiful things.

It's the time when we bring out of the garage (or out of the attic) the things we have stored for a year—things filled with memories. As we unwrap each ornament, we remember where it came from. As we string lights on a tree or hear a favorite song, we all feel what a song once called "gingerbread feelings."

But sometimes, if we are honest, the gingerbread is tinged with bitterness.

Perhaps our Christmas memories aren't so wonderful. Maybe each decoration we pull out reminds us of a painful past. Or maybe the hurt feels more real this time of year because everyone is supposed to feel joyful and happy and you're just feeling "meh."

Not quite depressed (although you may feel that).

Not quite happy (although you feel pretty good).

Even in the middle of your favorite carol, watching your favorite movie, or eating your favorite cookie (it's okay, holiday calories don't count), you're not feeling very joyful, definitely not peaceful, and maybe a little bit wondering exactly what went wrong.

While I love Christmas (a lot), I also am melancholy at heart.

I tear up frequently when I hear certain Christmas songs, and I often have to be reminded to smile as I sit and look at the 20 years of ornaments our family has put on the tree (over half of which I've had to move from the exact same branch). You can love Christmas and everything that it represents and still need a little reminder that all of the songs and sights and sounds add up to something more than you may remember.

Which is why I started sharing these thoughts on social media last Christmas.

Because I know I'm not alone. There are so many of us who love Christmas and the holiday season, but we need to be reminded that there is something more. That we are not alone. That it's okay to need a bit of help finding joy and peace during the holidays. That Christmas is the most wonderful time of the year not because Andy Williams sings about it, but because—well, you'll see.

So here we are.

Honestly, this book will read best if you start on December 1.

You can start whenever, but I recommend waiting until after Thanksgiving (don't be one of those people who try to rush Christmas*). Read this introduction, and then put it away until you're ready to start counting the days down until Christmas. Some of the entries are long, some of them are short and sweet, but all of them have a common purpose.

You won't find any partridges in pear trees here, but you may find something you don't expect: how to rest merry at Christmas.

*I won't judge if you are. I am also one of those people.

DECEMBER 1

You know one of my favorite things about Christmas?

The mess.

"Setting up" Christmas is messy because of all the storage boxes, the old tissue holding ornaments from your childhood, the musty-smelling decorations your grandma passed on to you that you can't get rid of.

It's messy because of the tree, and if you're doing it right, with a real live tree*, it's super messy. Getting it in the house means a trail of pine needles, spilled water as you try to balance it in the tree holder, and the cats who won't stop drinking out of it (or is that just at my house?).

*If you have a fake tree, see above about storage boxes and musty smells.

It's messy because of baking and cookies and dough everywhere and flour that seems to find itself into every crevice. Christmas is messy because of busy stores and crowded parking lots and kids spilling hot cocoa in the minivan.

It's messy because of wrapping paper and tape and boxes and all those delivery packages and kids eating candy canes during the holidays. Oh, and if you've got family to be with? Yeah, that can get messy, too.

But when Christmas is messy, it's actually perfect.

Because Christmas is all about finding God in the middle of the mess. He cares enough about the messy things in our world to literally put Himself right in the middle of it.

When the angel Gabriel appeared to Joseph (who was freaking out because his fiancée had just told him she was pregnant "by God"), the angel told him that Mary was going to have a baby, put there by God Himself. And Joseph was to name that baby Emmanuel, which is an old Hebrew word meaning "God with us."

Emmanuel.

We hear it a lot this time of year because of some old carols, but it's a word we don't use often any other time of year. Which is kind of sad, because Emmanuel is more than a name. It's a summation, a promise, a mind-altering reality.

God cares enough about the mess in this world.

He cares so much about your mess that He became "God with us."

Not God might be with us, or will be with us when we clean up our act. So don't be afraid of the mess. Don't worry if you're not good enough, your holiday won't look like one on the Hallmark Channel, and if your cookies look more like gingerbread blobs than gingerbread men. Your Christmas is going to be messy, which is actually a good—wonderful, in fact—thing.

God is okay with messy, because that's where He first revealed Himself to us.

Finding God in the middle of the mess is what Christmas is all about.

DECEMBER 2

Here you are, 23 days before Christmas and you're wondering, "Will I be okay?"

Yes. You will be okay.

Or, if you need it another way, try it like this.

YOU WILL BE OKAY.

Whatever you are facing, no matter how bad it looks, there is Someone bigger and greater than that thing you are scared of. And if you're like me, you've got lots of things that make you a little "nervous."

Maybe your thing is extra weight from too much egg nog and Diet Coke. Maybe you're worried about finances. Maybe your relationships are not going so well and the thought of spending an entire day with people who you don't even like very much right now has you freaked out. Maybe it's something much worse.

In times like those we all need to hear the words, "You are going to be okay."

I get it.

About ten years ago, I spent from Labor Day until just a couple weeks before Christmas unemployed. My job contract ended at the beginning of September, on the very day my youngest son was born. I started putting out my name, searching job boards. I must have sent out at least one thousand resumes, had hundreds of phone interviews, and met with close to one hundred people for interviews.

But nothing worked.

Nobody would hire me.

Everyone was friendly and loved me, but nobody would say, "You're hired."

It was a pretty dark time in my life, and I had some big fears. My youngest son was just a few months old when we came home from my parents' house one night to see our van getting repossessed. I will never be one of those people who loves God and says, "And then everything was perfect." Because I loved God more than most (probably), and my life still sucked.

I lost hope as we grew closer to Christmas, not just because I couldn't figure out exactly how we were going to pull off the presents, but because every time I thought I was about to get hired, I was rejected. It was hard to listen to my favorite Christmas songs that year, and although I love Andy Williams' Christmas music, if he'd walked into the house I may have punched him in his perfect 1960's crooner face.

I went to another interview at a large, nameless Northwest software company (you've probably never heard of it) and met with a really nice director. She was very kind and friendly and loved my resume and my experience but that's how everything had been for the last few months. Very nice people who seemed to thrive on soul-crushing rejection. I went home after the interview and honestly thought nothing more about it.

Then the phone rang.

It was her. She was calling to offer me a job. If she had said, "We want you to come clean toilets, but you'll be busy, because we have like a million of them here," I'd have been happy. I just wanted work. But she offered me something much better, and I remember my wife and I grabbing hands and doing something we rarely do: started dancing.

Why am I telling you all this?

Because I want you to know that I understand. Even when we get ready for the holidays, we can still face some really hard times. We can be listening to songs about flying reindeer and watch movies about elves and still be in the middle of a crisis that causes panic and worry and all the accompanying side effects.

That thing that is causing you to lose sleep or lash out or be angry and afraid? Through the Christmas story, God is reminding you that it's okay.

IT'S OK.

Yes, things may look bad.

Yes, all may not be perfect in your world.

But the story of Christmas is full of moments where heaven calms fragile, scared humans who were full of fear. In fact, when the angel first appears to the shepherds to tell them about Emmanuel's arrival, he does the same thing.

It's right there in the story. About to make an incredible announcement to a bunch of shepherds, the angel pauses. He sees the terror in their eyes. He can hear the quickness of their breath. He senses the fear and worry and does something amazing. He doesn't tell them not to freak out. He doesn't tell them to grow up and get a grip. He does what every loving person does to someone who is scared: offers reassurance.

Or, in less heavenly terms, he says, "It's going to be okay."

"But the angel reassured them. "Do not be afraid!" he said. "I bring you good news that will bring great joy to all people!" (Luke 2:10, NLT)

DECEMBER 3

Joy.

You don't see the word very much except at Christmas.

It's in the old song about "joy to the world" and it's on cards and decorations.

We even took a family picture by a giant JOY at the mall a couple years ago.

You may be asking yourself, "How can I be joyful in a year like this? How can there be joy in my heart when I watch the news or just happen to say the wrong thing to the wrong person on social media?" How can you be joyful when the kids are fighting, when there seems to be more month than there is money, when you're worried about _____(this is where you can fill in the blank with whatever your thing is).

If we were to be honest, this "most wonderful time of the year" fills a lot of us with worry and angst and fear. Maybe there's some sadness thrown in there, too. There's not a lot of room for joy, is there?

The trouble is that we think "joy" equals "happy."

And it doesn't.

The definition of joy is:

"Great delight or happiness caused by something exceptionally good or satisfying."

Wow. How often have you felt like that this year?

How many times have you honestly experienced something "exceptionally good or satisfying"? When was the last time you felt "great delight"?

(Another word we don't use very often, except at McDonald's, which has a breakfast sandwich using that word—but I don't think they honestly know what the word is supposed to mean. Have you tasted the "egg white delite"? Not very delightful, actually.)

Why does joy matter?

Why should we think about being joyful?

Because it's pretty important to God. In fact, the word joy appears 145 times in the Bible. In the New Testament, it appears 57 times. One New Testament writer uses the word and its various forms 16 times in one letter alone. God *wants* us to experience joy.

But honestly, when was the last time you felt something akin to joy?

When you got that raise? When you received the good report from the doctor? When you found out you were having twins? (I'm guessing on that one.)

We don't feel much joy because there's so much that comes along to take it away from us.

Bills.

Sickness.

Politics.

Family issues.

The list of joy-stealers would be long enough to fill several books, because they are different for every person. Different or not, we all have them. We all of things that make us look up at the sky and shake our fist and say, "How am I supposed to be happy now?"

It's not easy, but as you go through this book, I hope you discover how you can have joy in your world this Christmas. How to rest merry in the middle of the mess. The simplest answer?

You can have joy because there is a God.

There is a a God who loves you so much that He went to the greatest lengths possible for you to know Him. He left the glory of heaven for the confines of earth. The heart of the Christmas story is divinity wrapping itself in humanity—for *you*.

Those things that steal your joy? God cares about them. As one of the old carols reminds us, "He knows our need—to our weakness, no stranger."

God cares about the small stuff.

The big stuff.

And everything in between.

It's why Jesus came.

If we summed up everything behind Emmanuel's coming it can be summed up in that big idea: "I care so much about you that I want to be with you in every single thing you face. Big or small, good or bad, I will be with you." It's why He promised to never leave us or forsake us. It's why He promised that He would come back one day, so we could be with Him forever.

When something starts to rob you of your joy, remind yourself of those promises. When you start to get nervous or worried or afraid, remember the words of the angel to the shepherds:

But the angel reassured them. "Do not be afraid!" he said. "I bring you good news that will bring great joy to all people." Luke 2:10 (NLT)

DECEMBER 4

God knows exactly where you are today.

Right now, just a few weeks before Christmas, maybe you are ready to throw in the towel, ready to give up. You've lost heart. Your life has just gotten too messy. My friend, Jesus has something to say to you!

"But take heart! I have overcome the world." (John 16:33)

This is Jesus' way of saying "Rest you merry."

Yes, like in the old carol. "God Rest Ye Merry, Gentlemen," is a reminder that God wants us to feel this way during the holidays. (As an aside, the comma comes *after* the 'merry,' not before. God doesn't want the merry gentlemen to rest. He wants the gentlemen—and women, thank you very much—to rest merry.) But what does "rest merry" mean?

It's an archaic phrase meaning "be glad or joyful."

Imagine if we greeted everyone around us like this at Christmas! How much friendlier would the line at Starbucks be if, while waiting for your peppermint mocha, you looked at the harried mother in front of you and said, "Rest you merry! Let nothing you dismay!" (Sure, she might look at you like you were a bit crazy, but she will remember you and give her family a funny story to share.)

When Jesus told His friends that He had overcome the world, He was making something clear: the whole point of His coming at Christmas was to overcome all that is wrong in this fallen place. He stepped into our world, becoming one of us, so we could see that He understood and felt and had lived in the mess, too. He came into it so we would see that we didn't have to stay in the mess.

He was given the name Jesus because He came to save.

To save us from the world that is sometimes so hard to live in, so difficult to experience. He came to save us from the worst of ourselves, too. Our basest instincts and worst traits— our sinful, fallen selves. All those things that make us feel like giving up and quitting.

He deliberately showed up in a manger in the form of a baby to do one thing: overcome all of that. So take heart, because Jesus is saying this to you this Christmas season: "Be of good cheer, dear one! All is well."

Rest you merry.

Whatever you face today, my prayer is that you hear His voice and remember. Don't lose heart. Don't give up.

Let nothing you dismay—remember, Christ our Savior was born on Christmas Day!

DECEMBER 5

I have something shocking to tell you.

This may very well rock your entire understanding of the holiday.

The story of Christmas doesn't begin with a manger. And it doesn't begin with an angel showing up to tell a young girl she's going to have a baby. The story of Christmas begins long before, actually. Because the Christmas story begins at the beginning of all stories.

It begins shortly after Creation when two perfectly-created people in a perfect world willfully disobey God's one command, shattering the relationship between the Creator and His creation.

The very day that sin enters the world, God promises that a Savior, the Messiah, will come. He promises that He will send one who will break the chains of sin and death. He doesn't say when. He doesn't set a timetable. He only says that He will send someone.

Someday.

The entirety of the rest of the Old Testament can almost be summed up with one question, asked by Abraham, Jacob, Moses, Ruth, David, all the prophets. The question is woven through the entire narrative of kingdoms and battles and Psalms and queens and priests and temples. "When?" is the refrain. "When will God deliver us?"

And God's only answer is "Someday."

He gives hints, of course. In the prophetic books He talks about miraculous births and horrible deaths. He talks about the way the One will come, and He even speaks to Micah and tells exactly where this Savior will be born. (But nobody really pays attention, which explains a lot a few hundred years later.)

Then God stops speaking. He is silent and His people wonder when that promised day will come. For 400 years they wonder: "When?"

And suddenly, someday becomes today.

Someday finally comes when an angel appears to a young woman, delivering words from God, whose voice hasn't been heard in generations, telling her that "When" is now. And all of heaven pauses to hear her response.

"May it be to me just as you have said," says Mary.

The promise of a relationship with God comes to fruition, and what was fractured at time's beginning is forever healed. This is the Christmas story: the Creator loved His creation so much that He went to the greatest length possible to have a relationship with people like you and me.

But it's no longer "someday."

It's now.

Because He is here.

DECEMBER 6

Feeling overwhelmed this holiday season?

How about a little worried?

Maybe you've got anxiety?

Maybe a little of both? Like the storm that knocks out the power at the beginning of *Home Alone*, what should be the beginning of a happy wonderful season has turned into a crazed rush of emotions. (But check that you have all the kids before you go anywhere.)

Perhaps you feel overwhelmed because you think the thing you face is too big, too difficult, and impossible to overcome. You know the list of things that keeps you awake at night. You try to forget them in the busyness of the day, but nighttime comes and you lay in bed, waiting for them to visit you the way the Ghosts visited Ebenezer Scrooge. So what should be a joyful happy season just feels impossible.

If that's you today, I have good news!

You can rest merry, in spite of it all, because Christmas is *all about* impossible things.

Think about it! The story is nothing if not full of the improbably becoming probable, of the impossible being possible.

Angels show up everywhere.

An old man and woman who have *never* had children suddenly get pregnant and give birth to a son named John.

A girl becomes pregnant without ever having sex.

A fiancée marries a girl who he believes to be—to put it nicely, promiscuous (and is making crazy claims about how her baby came to be).

A Roman census puts a young couple precisely where they are supposed to be when her baby is born.

All the angels of heaven surprise shepherds and perform a glorious concert.

Magi follow one star across thousands of miles to an exact location prophesied about more than 1,000 years before.

Christmas is *filled* with moments when the impossible becomes possible.

All to remind you that your problem *isn't* impossible.

Take heart.

Take hope.

Be of good cheer.

Rest merry.

As the angel told Mary: "For nothing will be impossible with God." (Luke 1:37, NLT)

DECEMBER 7

You may have awakened today feeling much like the poet Henry Wadsworth Longfellow. He was one of the most famous Americans of the 1800's, and his poetry was known throughout the world. Famous for his works "The Midnight Ride of Paul Revere" and the epic *Song of Hiawatha*, he also lived profoundly touched by tragedy.

Around Christmas in 1863, the famous poet was feeling lost and torn and weary.

His wife of nearly 20 years had died only a few years before in a tragic fire. His country was racked by war, unrest, and political division at the height of the Civil War. As a staunch abolitionist, he was against slavery and all it stood for, but he abhorred the violence and death. He then received word that his oldest son had been severely wounded at the Battle of New Hope Church—he recovered, but his time as soldier was over.

That Christmas 1863, it all seemed too much for Longfellow.

Overwhelmed, burdened, and broken, the poet sat down and penned a poem called "Christmas Bells." In it, he expressed his heartbreak.

"In despair I bowed my head," he wrote. "There is no peace on earth, for hate is strong and mocks the song of 'peace on earth, goodwill to men.'"

Our world is not much different from Longfellow's. We live in a world that is filled with violence, anger, and death. Maybe the morning news has you feeling broken. Maybe personal tragedy or family heartache has you lost in dark thoughts. Maybe your finances are in shambles, your marriage in trouble, your kids in dire straits.

You may have bowed your head in despair today, too.

The fact that we have a traditional Christmas song that actually relates to where we are at today speaks volumes to me. Longfellow acknowledges that the ideas of peace on earth and goodwill to men seem nearly impossible in a world filled with hate. I can relate to feelings of despair and worry and doubt.

But Longfellow doesn't stop there.

Even in the midst of his darkest hour, the poet lifts his eyes. His heart begins to calm. "Then pealed the bells more loud and deep," he says.

God is not dead! He does not sleep!
The wrong shall fail, the right prevail,
With peace on earth, goodwill to men!

My prayer for you today: let your heart be lifted.

May you be filled with evidence everywhere that the One who came to us at Christmas is still here. He is not absent, He is not gone. He is not dead, nor does He sleep.

His very name, Emmanuel, says that wherever you are and whatever is happening in your life, He is here, and He promises that wrong will fail. Sin and death and destruction and all that is wrong with the world will not win. It cannot overcome the moment when all that was right came to be with us, wrapped in swaddling clothes and laid in a manger.

The horrible and awful things that caused you to bow your head today? They have lost. So lift your head and see the star and hear the message of the angels:

Emmanuel is here.

DECEMBER 8

I have bad news for you.

Resting merry takes a little bit of work.

You can't just think to yourself one morning during the holidays, "That old song about resting merry is right! I'm not gonna let anything dismay me!"

Because somehow, in some way, *something* is going to dismay you today.

You know, as I've already noted here, there's a lot of angst and messiness at Christmas. So when you think of resting merry, you have to actually put a bit of effort into it. The secret to finding joy and peace during the holidays actually takes a little bit of work on your part.

You're doing part of it just by reading this book. (Good job.)

But it takes more than just a little bit of time each day, thinking about the concepts of joy and peace and resting. Especially when the holidays are full of the tyranny of the urgent. You don't have time to sit and be quiet and rest and relax and just enjoy quiet moments, do you? When you look at your calendar for the holiday season, how much room did you leave for resting merry?

There's the kids' holiday concerts (if they go to public school) or Christmas concerts (if they go to Christian school). There's family parties (because you gotta keep the grandparents happy, am I right?). There's work parties (because you know that's the only way you'll get the extra gift cards and bonus check). Plus, you've got to get all the traditions in, so you've scheduled times for memories to be made.

Watch everyone's favorite movie? Check.

Bake the cookies? Check.

Read a great book about Christmas and resting merry? Check.

Gift exchange? Check.

Time to sit quietly in front of the Christmas tree, with the fire crackling, and quiet holiday songs playing in the background? "Uhm, maybe for ten minutes next Tuesday night, if we are home from the Peterson's house in time."

If you want to find joy and peace this Christmas, you've got to start saying no to a few things, lightening the schedule, and giving yourself room to just sit and be quiet. There's a reason so many great Christmas songs remind us about peace, and why the angels sang about "peace on earth." (It wasn't just so it would look good on a plaque on Etsy.) It's because God *really* wants you to pause in the middle of the craziness and think about what it all means.

When you do that, you're actually following part of the Christmas story that nobody talks about very often. You always get the shepherds and the inn and the manger and angels and the wise men. But rarely do we get the verse in Luke where Mary stops and just thinks about everything that just happened.

"But Mary kept all these things in her heart and thought about them often." (Luke 2:19 NLT)

After the noise of the town, the hustle and bustle of the too busy inn, the birth in the stable and the visit by the excited shepherds, Mary sat in quiet. She thought of everything that had happened that day, everything leading up to that moment. She held them closely and thought of them regularly.

Take some time to sit and be quiet.

Do it the next time you have a moment, after the crazy busyness.

Whether it's by the Christmas tree or somewhere else, follow the example of a woman who had every excuse for not taking time to sit and be still. If you want to find peace and joy, you'll need to spend less time thinking about all you need to get done and focus a bit more on what Christmas represents: what God already did.

DECEMBER 9

When you think of Christmas, what comes to mind?

Warm candlelight and fireglow. The smell of pine trees, gingerbread, and cinnamon. Presents beautifully wrapped, kids neatly pressed for pictures. But the reality of the Christmas story is less Hallmark than we'd like it to be.

We often forget how awfully terrible the birth of Jesus was. When we look at our nativity scenes, with cheerful people adoringly staring at a smiling happy baby in a manger, we forget the mess.

The mess of politics that drove the young couple from their home nearly 100 miles away to an overcrowded town at the whim of tax policy.

The mess of a barn filled with animals, their offspring, and the stench of urine and dung, and the lack of a clean, hygienic place to lay down.

The mess of a birth, with the pain and worry about the baby's health, the blood and the fluids, and nothing but straw and hay to sop it up.

The mess of a mother, exhausted, a father, dazed, both wondering if the baby they are holding, His red face contorted with tears, is truly what they believe Him to be.

The mess of a manger for a bed, with sheep pushing His swaddled body out of the way with their noses as they eat their dinner, angered by the little one's intrusion.

The mess of strangers, smelling even more like the worst parts of sheep, arriving and jostling for a view of the newborn, while the young couple looks on with confusion and maybe a little bit of fear.

Christmas, at its heart, is messy. Before we cleaned it up for cards and carols, it was rooted in the mess. It was dirty and smelly. It was crowded and uncomfortable. It's main characters weren't saints, but a scared man and woman grappling with the fact that there, in the middle of the mess, was God. That's what Christmas is really all about, after all: messy people in a messy world desperately needing someone to love them and save them right where they are, in the middle of the mess.

Wherever you are at today, Christmas is for you. Your life doesn't need to be cleaned up and picture perfect. You don't have to put on a smile or pretend like the world around you doesn't stink, that your life isn't freaking you out a bit. Like Mary and Joseph, you may be nervous or scared or worried or confused. That's ok, my friend!

God really does show up in the middle of the mess.

DECEMBER 10

Unexpected news?

A bill you didn't see coming?

Health issues for someone you love?

Relationships strained?

I get it. It's hard any time of the year, but worse at Christmas. You may think you're alone with the hard things this season, but it just takes a glance across your friends' social media posts to realize you're not. The season of light and hope can sometimes feel like the season of pain and worry and stress.

"He knows our need, to our weakness no stranger."

These words from the French Christmas hymn "Cantique de Noël" " have always resonated with me. In English, "O Holy Night" is a song that beautifully focuses on the Incarnation—God becoming man. Christmas is about us encountering a God who wasn't removed or distant. When we look at the baby in the manger, we see a God who is *just like us*.

Yes, Jesus was fully God and eternal and had been there at Creation and had walked with Moses and Elijah. The God part was inherent to His very being: all-powerful, all-wise, all-encompassing.

But the Incarnation says that God *limited* Himself. When He wrapped Himself in our flesh and blood, He took on the limitations of our humanity. He grew tired. He got hungry.

As a baby, He had to learn to talk and crawl. He had to learn how to feed himself, wash His face, and all the rest. But beyond that, He wasn't just doing human things. He was fully human, so He felt what humans feel. He had parents who stressed out over finances. He had friends with health concerns. He grew up amidst political turmoil and religious strife. He knew what it was like to lose friends, have bad family relationships, and watch people He loved die.

He was fully God, yes.

But fully human, too.

Divinity clothed in humanity.

Which means He knows exactly what you're facing right now. Intimately, deeply, and personally. He knows the weakness of doubt and worry and fear, because He lived and loved and walked in a world filled with it.

But it also means that you can trust Him.

You can lean into Him, cry out to Him, rail at Him, and rest in Him. He knows your need. Why don't you tell Him what it is and trust that He will help you deal with it in ways you can't understand now?

He won't keep you at arm's length. The Incarnation shows that He longs to be close, to draw you near. And when you're wrapped in Him, He will remind you, gently, "I am here, beloved. Calm your heart. As I was near to the Father, I am near to you. Rest in my heavenly peace."

DECEMBER 11

Last year I realized our vents needed to be cleaned.

The closer we got to Christmas, the colder the house seemed to get. So I called a local company and had them send over a technician.

He was incredibly thorough. He did a great job and saved me from having to get a new furnace by cleaning out the fan and the rest of the main assembly. His name was Simon, and as he worked, I talked to him about the holidays. He noticed my Christmas music playing on the front porch (yes, I keep a speaker out there and stream Christmas music all day and all night so it feels festive when you approach the house).

It turns out that Simon was actually Jewish. I asked him about Hanukkah and what his family did for their traditions, and he asked me about our Christmas traditions. When he finished, we sat down at the dining room table and kept talking. We talked about our journeys.

As we sat there, we encouraged each other in our faiths, even though they diverge at the book of Malachi. God used this man's faith to encourage and challenge me as a father, husband, and in my own faith. I was in a pretty unhappy place that day. I was worried about my health, my finances.

Simon honestly spoke words of life into me in that moment.

We didn't have a lot in common. But because he asked me about my Christmas music, we ended up finding a deep connection over our stories and journeys and the way God will direct and guide us to where He wants us to be.

There's an old English poem that speaks about a stranger coming into the house. The stranger blesses the man and his house and all that is important to him, and goes on his way.

Then a lark sings, "Often goes Christ in the stranger's guise."

At Christmas, the idea of God being in a stranger's guise is not uncommon. The fact that He came as He did, unexpected and unlooked for, means the baby Jesus truly was a stranger. And yet, when He came into the world, He changed it forever.

He left an indelible mark, helping people understand their stories and journeys and the way God calls us and gently leads us to Him.

Simon called himself my Christmas miracle that day. We've spoken off and on since that day, encouraging each other, wishing each other well. He blessed my house and all that was important to me on that day a few weeks before Christmas.

And the lark sang, "Often, often, often, goes Christ in the stranger's guise."

(The American composer Alfred Burt set this poem to music in 1943. It's a beautiful carol.)

DECEMBER 12

When God is busy working, He doesn't usually let us see what He is doing.

He operates out of time, and we, in our constant watching of the clock, begin to worry and wonder what He is up to.

It can even be a little scary.

The story of Christmas shows that over and over again. God is doing something big, and it scares Zechariah, Elizabeth, Mary, and Joseph. It terrifies the shepherds and even wakes the wise men from their sleep.

But God goes out of His way, every time, to reassure them.

He's doing the same thing today, for you, dear friend.

"They were terrified, but the angel reassured them. "Don't be afraid!" he said." (Luke 2:9b-10a, NLT)

God knows that uncertainty is scary.

He knows that we do not like the unexpected. Humans love to plan ahead and be prepared for the worst (anyone remember Y2K?), but that doesn't stop us from freaking out when things don't go the way we think they should.

When the angels show up, they freak the shepherds out.

They were *terrified*.

They felt "extreme fear." The synonym here is *petrified*. What they saw gave them stupefying fear so great they couldn't move. One minute they are watching a bunch of sheep and the next they are certain it's the end.

The angel knows it's not the end.

The angel knows he's there to give them the best news ever.

But he doesn't say that to them.

He doesn't give them all the reasons why their fear is unfounded or why they are dumb to feel that way. The word that Luke uses for what the angel *did* do? It's perfect.

The angel *reassures* them.

Reassure is a word that means "to say or do something to remove doubts or fears." It's what you do to your child when they are wounded and scared and convinced the blood dripping from their head means they are going to die. My youngest daughter went through this exact moment a few years ago. Playing at a friend's house, she put a pogo stick up in a treehouse (the reasoning behind this decision remains uncertain) and it fell out and landed on her head. Blood and chaos and tears ensued.

As I drove her to the emergency room, I didn't tell her she'd made a bad choice. I didn't tell her all the reasons why she shouldn't have put a pogo stick in a treehouse. She saw the blood and was only concerned about one thing. "Daddy," she asked, "Am I going to die?" The only thing she needed from me? Reassurance. My job right then was "to say or do something to remove doubts or fears." (She's ok. But she wants me to tell you *not* to put pogo sticks in treehouses.)

The angel was in a similar situation with the shepherds. He knows in their current state they aren't ready for the good news of great joy. So he stops and reassures them. "Don't be afraid! It's going to be ok! Trust me!"

When God is at work, when we face the unexpected, when we can't tell what He is up to, it's ok. If you are afraid or nervous or scared, He reassures you the way the way the angel reassured the shepherds: "Don't be afraid! You have favor with me." He says, "It's going to be okay. Ok?"

DECEMBER 13

Every year, on Christmas Eve, I read Charles Dickens' best-loved book.

A Christmas Carol. In Prose. Being a Ghost Story of Christmas is one of my favorite books of all time, and ever since I was in high school, I've read the book all the way through on Christmas Eve.

(In honesty, I don't get through the whole book anymore. With kids and getting ready for the next day, I don't have enough time, so I have a good substitute—but I'll get to that shortly.)

You know the story. It's been adapted into countless versions and whether your favorite version stars the Muppets or Bill Murray or Mickey Mouse or Alastair Sim, you know the basic story, and honestly for a story that says "Merry Christmas!" so often and speaks about the good Christmas does for the world, it's a pretty bleak tale. (It actually starts reminding us that one of the characters is dead, and we better understand that, okay?)

Why do I bring up this classic holiday tale in a book about finding joy and peace at Christmas? Besides the fact that the caroler outside Scrooge's counting house actually sings "God rest ye merry, gentlemen?" It matters because you aren't going to find peace and joy at Christmas if you've got the attitude of Ebenezer Scrooge.

You may not be a miserly old man, but if you look at the story closely, you can see some of Scrooge's fatal flaws which lead him to his ghostly visits on Christmas Eve. What leads him to this life of anger, bitterness, and resentment? What has caused him to push the holiday so far away that his nephew observes that Scrooge doesn't even observe it anymore?

Some of Scrooge's hurts may sound familiar.

Bad family situation growing up.

Distant father.

Financial insecurity.

Worry about the future.

Lost love.

Loneliness.

Scrooge's bitterness and bah humbugs don't come from nowhere. They are deeply rooted in his past and have caused him to have no peace, no joy, and no room for Christmas.

You may not be in that place yet. Maybe you haven't fully succumbed to hoping anyone who wishes you a "Merry Christmas" is buried with a stake of holly in their heart. But maybe you are having trouble finding joy and peace—maybe you aren't resting merry—because you've let things like bitterness and anger and resentment take hold of you.

I want to encourage you to see what you can do to give up the hurt before the holidays progress much further. Scrooge is shown the error of his ways by four ghosts, but I'm hopeful it won't take that for you.

If you need to forgive someone today, go do it.

Something you're bitter about? Find a way to root it out.

"No space of regret can make amends for one's life's opportunity misued," writes Dickens. *A Christmas Carol* is a great little book, and it has done wonders to help make the celebration of the season what it is today. But it's nothing compared to what actually happened at Christmas. Jesus came at Christmas to free us from the worst of ourselves, and to be there, right alongside us, when we face the difficult moments.

All the things you struggle with, that cause people to think of you as a bit of a Scrooge? It's time to deal with them. Wake up, like Scrooge did, and resolve to be a different person and make things right.

"Really, for a man who had been out of practice for so many years it was a splendid laugh!" is said of Scrooge, but hopefully it can be said of you, too, this Christmas.

If you really want to see the best version of Dickens' story, check out George C. Scott's 1984 version. Released theatrically in Europe and shown on CBS in the United States, it's a stellar adaptation and one of the most faithful to the original tale.

DECEMBER 14

I can hear a Christmas carol playing while I sit here in Starbucks.

I think I'm the only person listening to the words, which are full of the Good News.

There are people reading newspapers, talking to each other, arguing over something political. A guy is texting his pals, while a woman just complained about what someone posted on her Facebook profile. They are drinking coffee, picking up mobile orders, and everyone is either in a hurry or completely preoccupied with the world we live in to notice the message being sung to them.

It's not much different than it was when Jesus was born.

Nobody noticed.

Nobody heard.

Nobody paid attention.

The Roman soldiers overseeing the census didn't care that Joseph and Mary couldn't find a place to sleep, nor that she was ready to have a baby—unless perhaps to note it on the tax form.

The innkeeper isn't mentioned in the story, but somebody had to make clear that there was no room in the inn. His space was filled up already, with no room for a couple from Nazareth ("Can anything good come from Nazareth?" was a familiar saying at the time). We know that somehow, Joseph hears "No room in the inn" and scrambles.

His wife is about to have a baby.

They are literally ignored by everything and everyone around them.

Nobody cares.

So Joseph makes do the best he can. He finds where the animals are being sheltered and takes his wife there. It's not what he intended. He was a carpenter after all. He probably envisioned a handmade cradle for his newborn son in a clean house he'd built for them with his own hands.

He looks at the hay. He smells the urine and dung. He looks at Mary. He wants to say something, but doesn't have time. She looks at him and gasps and what has been promised since the Garden suddenly begins. She falls to the ground and he does his best to help while all of Bethlehem ignores the cries and shouts and tears.

The baby is born. The Savior has come.

And nobody notices.

If the heavenly hosts hadn't shown up to celebrate the birthday, even the shepherds would have stayed in the fields. Imagine, the moment when eternity stepped into humanity, and the only witnesses were a dazed young man, an exhausted young woman, and several men smelling of sheep.

The shepherds left and told everyone what they saw and the Bible says that everyone who heard their words were amazed. It does *not* say, "Everyone who heard their words believed them and went and saw the baby for themselves."

Even after they are told by eye witnesses.

Even after the shepherds tell them about the angels and the baby and the "good news of great joy," people respond with only "Wow! Amazing!" and then turn right back to whatever they were doing before. They still do not notice.

My prayer for you this Christmas is that you will have time to notice.

Take time to pause, and hear the message of hope, the promise of personal peace, the announcement of joy that came to us the night that Christ was born.

May the familiar words of the story, the refrains of the carols, cause you to pause--to listen--and hear Good News.

"Joy to the world! The LORD has come!"

DECEMBER 15

I visited a dear friend last Christmas.

Christmas music played, and her tree was lit.

She sat near the kitchen table, and I know I saw an elf nearby. In spite of the elf and the tree and the Christmas music, this was not a house full of holiday cheer. It was a place where there are more questions than answers, more worry than joy, and the exhaustion on her face showed that she was tired of the fight.

All I could do was walk up to her, hold her hand in mine, and lean close. That's when the tears ran down our cheeks. This is not how our year started. This is not what we expected to happen. She feels helpless and hopeless, and I didn't want to offer her platitudes and meaningless words. Her pain is deep, her wounded heart, broken because those who should rally behind her and lift her up have all but left her alone.

The friends who joined me in the visit helped bring a much-missed smile to her face.

It was clear that in spite of all that has happened, it meant everything that we were near.

Which is why the only words I could truly utter, over and over again, were "Emmanuel, God With Us." My dear friend needs the ones who love her to be there, beside her, to lift her up in prayer when her own prayers no longer come easily. And hopefully, we helped her remember that the One who loves her is even closer. It's what his name means—it's His very nature: the God who is near.

This is one of the struggles of Christmas, isn't it?

We want everything to be merry and bright, but there is pain and suffering. We want to say, "All is well," but we can't because we are in the middle of hell. Maybe this story hits close to home because this where you are today. Maybe you are too hurt, too broken, too full of pain to feel any gingerbread feelings. You feel only the pain and need something to calm the hurt and make it feel better. If it's not you, maybe it's someone you love, and you're wondering, "What can I do?"

Sometimes, the only think you can do is to do what I did that day.

"Emmanuel. God With Us."

Say it again. And again.

Then say it again and remind yourself that you are not alone. You don't face the darkness without light shining because of His coming. He is here. He is with us. And whatever you face today, I pray that you will feel His presence and know the power of Emmanuel.

Emmanuel. God with us.

God with *you.*

DECEMBER 16

If one watched only the news and read only what people shared on social media, one might be hard-pressed to find joy in the holiday season. I even heard a prominent Christian author say that she was having a hard time celebrating last year because the world is such a mess.

(Spoiler alert: it's not getting better.)

It's very easy to complain about how bad everything is, how messy the world has become. But when we do that, we minimalize the power of the Incarnation and what Jesus' coming actually means to us, today.

If we truly believe what we say we believe about Christmas (you know, the key part being that *God Himself took on human form and became one of us*), then our attitude about how bad the world is should change. You don't have to put on rose-colored glasses and pretend that everything is hunky dory, but you do need to see the coming of Christ for what it actually is and means to us right now.

Remember, Christmas is all about finding the best in the middle of the worst. The Incarnation is Jesus coming to give us what we most desperately need.

Need peace in your life and wish there was more in the world at large?

The "prince of peace" is resting in the manger.

Are you wondering where your life is headed and wish someone would give you direction?

The Baby wrapped in swaddling clothes is the "wonderful counselor."

If you're concerned over issues of justice and mercy, remember He said He came to "set the oppressed free."

If you worry about your finances, He promised that His Father would care for you and provide what you need.

Has your health got you down? Take heart, because He "healed all kinds of sickness and all kinds of disease among the people."

Whatever your situation or frame of mind, you can find hope, joy, peace, healing, comfort, rest, and yes, salvation, in Jesus. The trouble with most of us who believe in Jesus is that we relegate His salvation to the end. We think only of what happens after we die and accept that He saved us from our sins because He wants us to be in heaven with Him.

That is not why He came.

Christmas is *not* about you getting into heaven when you die.

Jesus explained why He came.

"My purpose is to give them a rich and satisfying life." (John 10:10, NLT)

So if you're feeling overwhelmed by anything, remember why He came at Christmas. Whatever your worry or fear or concern, Jesus came to either deal with it or give you the strength to deal with it.

He didn't just come to save you from your sins so you could one day have eternal life in heaven, He literally came to save us from everything that resulted from that fateful decision in Eden. The Incarnation is all eternal life—life that lasts forever.

Which starts today.

Abundant, overflowing *life*.

Because He came at Christmas.

DECEMBER 17

Resting merry.

How's it going in the eight days before Christmas?

It's okay if you're still working on it.

I'm not an expert on it yet, either, and it's something I've been trying to do for nearly all my adult life. Which may explain why I am so obsessed with Christmas music. I've been collecting it since I was in college. Today, my iTunes library has 12,125 Christmas songs in it. That's 27 days' worth of music, all different versions of many of the same songs. A couple hundred versions of "Silent Night" or "Chestnuts Roasting on an Open Fire" or "Jingle Bells."

I honestly love hearing fresh takes on Christmas songs. When I hear something I know by heart and it surprises me or gives me a new twist on something I've heard hundreds of times, I pause and rewind and listen again.

Which is kind of what resting merry requires.

To find joy and peace at Christmas, you may need to look at what has become overwhelming familiar in a new way. To find the surprise in the sameness, to find magic in the mundane.

Like this example of the song that inspired the title of this book, "God Rest Ye Merry, Gentlemen."

The original lyrics are archaic and familiar.

God rest ye merry, gentlemen, let nothing you dismay!

Remember, Christ our Savior was born on Christmas Day

To save us all from Satan's power when we had gone astray!
Oh, tidings of comfort and joy!
Tidings of comfort and joy!

You've heard it so often at the holidays you probably even knew a lot of the words. You've probably heard the Christmas story so often you can quote it by heart and have most of it memorized. So try a new take on the familiar. See it differently and it may help you find what is sorely missing: surprise.

May God give you rest and peace, dear friends.
Don't be worried or afraid.
Remember, Christ the Savior was born on Christmas for one purpose:
To save us—all of us—from the power of the evil one, who leads us away from our hope and joy.

Sometimes an old carol, seen in a new way, can encourage you. With just a week before the celebration of His coming, I hope you are able to look at the traditional and familiar and see it for what it truly is: the greatest moment in history, when divinity wrapped itself in humanity, when God came near.

Rest merry.

Don't be afraid.

DECEMBER 18

Christmas is the season of light and hope.

It's the celebration of that moment in time when heaven and earth met—when God wrapped himself in humanity and became not a conquering hero, but a tiny, helpless baby. Just one child among millions born into this world.

And yet, this one child is the One Child that cannot be forgotten or ignored.

History is full of moments when its course was forever changed because just one child was born.

Imagine, for just a moment, what the world would have been like if Jonas Salk had never been born—we might never have found a vaccine for polio—and millions of children might still be suffering from that disease today.

Imagine a world without Abraham Lincoln. We might be living still in a divided nation—half slave, half free. Without the birth of Julius Caesar, there would have been no Roman empire, without Guttenberg, no printing press.

Of course our nation's recent history, history that remains in our collective consciousness, was forever changed because of just one child's birth. A child that grew up to hijack a plane—a child that grew up to be a rescue worker. We can picture these people and realize that our lives have been changed because these people were born.

You see, one child can make a difference in this world.

One Child has made *the* difference in this world.

That One Child, Jesus Christ, who came to earth not just to affect human history and change the world—but to affect *your* history and change *your* life. This One Child, born in an obscure village in a tiny corner of the Roman empire, became the centerpiece of all history. Our calendars are based on His birth. Every year the entire world stops and celebrates His arrival.

Oh, it gets a bit more obscured every year.

"Happy Holidays" and eliminations of the name of the actual day are just more obvious attempts to pretend that His birth doesn't matter. And yet, for all of the obscuring, for the attempts to wipe away the word "Christmas," it is still there. Obvious. Obscure it all you want, it won't be ignored.

Why?

Because this One Child was born to do something no other child was born to do:

To give hope to the hopeless.

To give joy to the joyless.

To be a friend to those in need. This Child grew up to be the Man who changed the world—the Man who conquered death with life and stands ready today, ready to tell you that your life does matter—that you do make a difference—and that His love is all you need.

As this year's celebration of His birth draws close, I pray that your life will be impacted–and perhaps changed–by the One Child who forever changed the world.

DECEMBER 19

Are there small things stealing your joy this holiday season?

Maybe it's the long lines and crabby people in the stores.

Is it the cheesy music on the radio? (How dare you insult my favorite genre of music? Now you've stolen *my* joy!)

Perhaps you're irritated by family?

Or the kids already out of school and driving you crazy?

Or the cold weather?

Or the fact that you won't get anything you actually want for Christmas this year?

There are literally hundreds of things every day that steal joy. The struggle is overcoming those little things and saying to yourself what the apostle Paul says in Philippians:

"I will continue to rejoice." (Philippians 1:18 NIV)

"For I know that as you pray for me and the Spirit of Jesus Christ helps me, this will lead to my deliverance." (Philippians 1:19 NLT)

Paul understood things stealing joy. By the time he wrote these words to the believers in Philippi, he was living chained to a Roman guard. He'd been beaten, unfairly imprisoned, shipwrecked, stoned and left for dead. And yet, he says, "I will continue to rejoice."

Paul has confidence in the outcome of his situation. No matter how bleak it is, no matter what ominous turn it may take, he is confident that God's will shall be done, and it will turn out for his good.

I wish I had confidence like that. Especially at Christmas*.

See list of irritations. And I'm still a little miffed about how you feel about Christmas music.

Life is messy.

Life is irritating.

It's frustrating.

But it shouldn't be soul-stealing.

Someone once said, "Don't sweat the small stuff." But then the small stuff piles up and *then* the big stuff happens. And joy goes out the window.

So, today, do your best to keep track of the irritations. Write them down, ask yourself what is it that is bugging you, and then, remember that Jesus' birth at Christmas actually gives you the ability and power to overcome the irritations. Like Paul, you can have deliverance from the things that drag you down.

You can have joy.

And the next time something really bugs you and causes you to lose it, don't just sing "Joy to the world." Say what Paul said—"I will rejoice constantly"—and choose joy this Christmas.

DECEMBER 20

I love reading Christmas books and watching Christmas movies.

I love the decorations and the lights and the music and the stories of joy and love and happiness and things working out beautifully with snow falling just as the story ends and the credits roll.

The most popular network on television during Christmas is the Hallmark Channel. Every day for nearly two months, they show movies about small towns and big companies and improbably beautiful people falling in love just in time for the holidays.

I must confess, I enjoy watching them. Sure they are predictable and a bit cheesy, but who wouldn't enjoy a Christmas that is greeting card perfect? Trouble is, even when there is conflict in these stories, they don't get messy enough.

And part of the secret of resting merry at Christmas is finding God in the middle of the mess. Which is why, although I can enjoy the Hallmark Channel Christmas movies, they aren't the ones that resonate most with me. My favorites are the ones that are a bit more—real.

Christmas Vacation.

A Christmas Story.

A Charlie Brown Christmas.

Rudolph, the Red-Nosed Reindeer.

It's a Wonderful Life.

The plots can be summarized pretty easily.

A dysfunctional family celebration goes from bad to worse to horrific to up in flames.

A kid wants *one* perfect gift for Christmas and everyone tells him it will blind him.

A boy tries to find meaning in the holiday and is mercilessly mocked by his friends.

A misfit is disowned by his dad, mocked by Santa Claus, and kicked out of society.

A man with dreams lives a selfless life and decides to commit suicide on Christmas Eve.

When you summarize the Christmas classics this way, you may wonder why we allow our children to watch them and why we get them out and watch them every year. Honestly, it's because we can relate so well. We *are* annoyed by our families. We *don't* always get what we wish for. Sometimes the people we care about most are unkind. And reality often gets in the way of our hopes and dreams.

I watch these movies every year because I relate to them a lot more than I care to admit. I want to think of myself as a jolly old Santa Claus this time of year, but honestly am a lot more like Clark Griswold.

I feel you, Ralphie. I get it, Charlie Brown. I've been there, Rudolph.

And George Bailey, when you lose it on your entire family and ask your wife, "Why'd we have to have all these kids?" as you desperately wonder how you'll recover from a dark day—that is literally me. (My kids watched the movie and said so. Ouch.)

And when your joy is gone, it doesn't just hurt you.

It hurts everyone around you.

Because people without joy are hard to be around. Even at Christmastime.

Which is why Paul's encouragement from Philippians is so timely and important.

"Rejoice in the Lord always." (Philppians 4:4 NIV)

Always. It means constantly.

You can rejoice when the cable goes out during the football game.

You can rejoice when your kids won't stop annoying you.

You can rejoice when you get bad news from the doctor.

You *can* rejoice—always.

And this holiday season would be a great time to start.

Ask God to help you rejoice, especially when you don't feel like it. When things get crazy and hectic this holiday, don't give in to your inner George Bailey. Pause, stop, and remind yourself that Jesus came and his arrival was meant to fill your world with "great joy."

DECEMBER 21

It's not easy to find peace at Christmastime.

Which is a bit ironic, since it's literally in the first Christmas song. (The one the angels sang at Jesus' birth.) And one of the titles for Jesus is "Prince of Peace." And you can buy Christmas cards with the word embossed in gold under a picture of your children looking quiet and clean for the only time the entire year.

But if we look around we don't feel very peaceful.

The world is not at peace.

Our homes are not peaceful.

And maybe you're not even at peace with yourself.

The trouble is we think *peace* means an absence of war or being free from internal strife. But that's not what the angels meant when they sang "Glory to God in the highest, and on earth peace, good will toward men." (Luke 2:14, KJV) It's not what Jesus meant when He talked about peace.

The biblical idea of peace is bigger, grander, and far more wonderful. It comes from a Hebrew word, *shalom,* which actually means "to be complete." In other words, God doesn't want us to just get along with others. He wants us to be *complete or whole.* He wants us to *live well.*

Who doesn't long for that?

We do everything we can to have better health.

We eat right, we exercise, we drink a "skinny" version of our favorite drink in hopes that it might rub off on us. We do everything we can to have better relationships. We read books, we go to seminars, we take online quizzes to ensure we know how we're supposed to get along with our spouse.

We do everything we can to have a great career. We improve our job performance, we listen to our supervisors, we look for the next great opportunity to make more money, get a better position.

And yet we aren't at peace.

We aren't complete at all.

Our lives are—messy.

Because we've missed the point.

Jesus didn't come to the world to make everyone get along. He came to give us what He himself said was different than what we expected.

"Peace I leave with you, my peace I give you. I do not give as the world gives. Do not let your hearts be troubled and do not be afraid." (John 14:27, NIV)

Not as the world gives.

It's not temporary. It's not for just a moment.

It's more than just everyone getting along.

Jesus offers something more. Something bigger and greater.

Think of that for just a moment.

The God of the universe, the One who created the sun and moon and stars, the One who oversees time and space cares about YOU so much, that He wants you to be complete. He longs for you to be whole. This is why He reminds you that your life can be untroubled, and why you don't have to be afraid.

Jesus says the only way to find peace is in Him.

Peace—living full and well and complete—is found nowhere else. It's why He came at Christmas. It's why He was born.

DECEMBER 22

I have something to say that will probably shock you.

You may want to be sitting down if you aren't already.

Ok. Here it is:

Your family Christmas will not be whatever you are expecting it to be.

Just to make sure you get it: *your family Christmas will not be what you want it to be.*

I know. I'm sorry to disappoint you.

But it's true.

After nearly 50 years of Christmases, I've come to realize that in spite of all the preparation, all of the planning and the work, it's just not going to be what I expect.

You won't all be happy at the same time.

Not everyone will like the food you worked so hard to cook.

Every present will not be a home run.

You will have the holiday you have, in spite of all your efforts.

Let that sink in for just a moment. It's not what you want to hear, I know. You've scoured the Pinterest boards, read the books, did the research on the best means of exterior lighting. But none of that will lead to the *perfect Christmas.*

Let me give you an example.

True story—one holiday my mom made a pumpkin pie and it looked amazing. It was a thing of beauty, and I *love* pumpkin pie. It's a huge weakness of mine. And my mom, being my mom, knew that. We walked into my parents' house and she had a beautiful slice just sitting there, whipped cream at the ready. "Here's your fork," she said. I took the fork, dove into that pumpkin pie and took a huge bite.

It was horrible.

It didn't taste like pumpkin pie.

It tasted like pumpkin on crust with a bit of old cinnamon thrown in.

With the bite still on my tongue, I said, "It's not sweet."

"What?"

"It's not sweet. Not sweet. Not sweet!" and I spit it out.

My mom forgot the sugar. (And to be clear, this was the *only* time her pumpkin ever tasted horrible. Sorry for exposing you, mom.) It looked like a perfect pie, it smelled like it, and it had the texture of it. But it wasn't pumpkin pie because it was missing that crucial ingredient.

Your *perfect Christmas* won't happen because no matter how hard you try, it's missing one ingredient: perfection.

We are flawed, frail people living in a fallen world. We won't have the perfect holiday because *we* aren't perfect.

And it's ok, my friend.

It's okay!

Here's the good news: God gave you the family you have. He went through the same year you did. And *nothing* that happens surprises Him.

Your Christmas will be—well, messy. But that's ok. If Christmas teaches us anything, it's that God is found in the middle of the mess.

(But honestly don't forget the sugar in the pumpkin pie.)

DECEMBER 23

All the excitement leading to the big day is building.

The anticipation is off the charts, and there are hushed whispers everywhere. Eyes light up at the thought of all the joy that will be shared, and everywhere there's that feeling one gets when waiting nearly for forever for the day to finally arrive!

It's even more exciting because the gift is so unexpected.

Sure, everyone knows the gift is coming, but nobody knows how it will be wrapped, and even when they look hard for it, they aren't ever going to find it, because it's been hidden in a most unexpected place.

This is how it feels around my house today.

We know the day is near.

We can sense it. But we aren't sure exactly how it will all play out, and there's so much to be excited about.

I'm certain this is how heaven felt in the moments leading up to His birth.

While Mary and Joseph were anxious and nervous about what was coming, heaven was filled with energy, excitement, and wonder. The best gift ever was about to be delivered, and while the whole world had been told it was coming, nobody knew what it would look like.

This is the joy and excitement and wonder of Christmas.

May you feel some of that same anticipation today, as you look toward the holiday. Whether surrounded by family or alone, the gift that came that day was for you, too.

The best gift ever, given on the best night ever, so you can have the best life ever.

DECEMBER 24

It's the day before.

There is still so much to do, and you may still be struggling with resting merry.

I get it. You have a lot of memories to cram into the next 48 hours. You have emotions to feel, pictures to take, social media posts to share, and presents to wrap. (Surely I'm not the only one who still wraps some presents on Christmas Eve?) The stockings are hung by the chimney with care, I'll bet, and you're probably looking forward to the moment when the children get nestled all snug in their beds and dream of sugarplums. (A weird dream, but I digress.)

So, to get you ready to rest, I want to encourage you to take some time to find your favorite collection of Christmas songs. Maybe you rightly recognize that *The Andy Williams Christmas Album* is the greatest Christmas album ever. You might be a fan of *Mannheim Steamroller Christmas*. Your tastes may lean toward one of Michael W. Smith's many Christmas collections or you may enjoy something with a bit more of a retro feel: *Funky Funky Christmas* by New Kids on the Block. (Shame on you.)

There are literally *thousands* of Christmas albums. You may have some family favorites that bring back great memories (I'm partial to the old *Reader's Digest* Christmas LP's) and you can choose from country, choral, bluegrass, jazz, pop, swing, heavy metal, rap, house, dance, rock. Every style of music has its Christmas collection, and every year artists put out their holiday albums in the hopes that they will be the next Bing Crosby (not a chance).

So find the one you like best—just make sure it's got some carols on it.

You see, there's a reason why it'd be a good idea to spend a few moments—maybe even a full thirty minutes—to just sit and listen to all these familiar songs that you know nearly every word to, even though you only listen to them a few weeks out of the year.

Today, the familiar is necessary.

You see, you've have heard the songs a million times already, and unlike most songs about God and His love for humanity, these familiar songs speak to the heart. The beauty of the familiar is calling to you.

Songs you know.

Melodies you can sing.

Warm gingerbread feelings everywhere.

Maybe in these songs, you can find what is hidden in plain sight. Maybe they can help you see the Story you've already known for years.

Jesus was born.

He came at Christmas.

And He did it because He loves you and wants you to have the best life ever.

There is great beauty in the old words, some written by great theologians and some written to teach theology. They help us understand why the angels sang on high, why gentlemen (and women) can be merry and not dismayed, and why He came upon a midnight clear.

Let the carols remind you of the Story, full of joy and richness, that maybe we can only truly understand once a year, in the quiet of Christmas Eve.

The angels helped the shepherds find the Savior in the middle of the mundane, the boring, and the familiar.

As you listen today, may you do the same.

I have included a few suggestions for great listening at the end of the book. If you need ideas for some great Christmas music, please take a look. And please, no New Kids on the Block.

CHRISTMAS DAY

Merry Christmas!

You made it to the best day of the year!

Before it gets too crazy (or maybe the kids are already awake and you can just get them to wait for a few more minutes), this would be a great time to remember to *rest merry*.

Don't let the day overwhelm you.

Don't let your expectations for how it should go defeat you.

Don't forget to choose to be joyful.

And when you need a bit of peace and the house is too crazy, go hide in the bathroom and regroup.

Beyond all that, though, it's here.

And it's not a day about trees and trimmings.

It's not really about presents or delicious food or friends and family.

Today is about you.

Well, you and the baby who was born on this day.

He did it for you.

Because He knew you would struggle with the worst of yourself. Because He knew you would need to be reminded that you are loved—that you matter—that you have a purpose. He doesn't care that you don't like every Christmas song, or that your stuffing looks more like gravy. He doesn't care that your wrapping paper doesn't match, that your best efforts would still be a Pinterest fail, that you still don't know what a yule log is.

God looks at you and all your faults and failings and loves you anyway.

It's the reason He came at Christmas.

There's a reason the whole world stops for a moment on this day. Because on this particular day, heaven and earth met. On this day, God went from being far and distant and spoken to only through priests and prophets to something so completely different that we must pause and reflect on it.

In other words, there's a lot of reasons to be joyful at Christmas. But it's not always easy. It's not always Hallmark Channel perfection, and it may not look good on the annual family Christmas card. And maybe that's your life this Christmas Day. Then just remember this: you can have joy and peace, because if you look closer at the messy manger, you'll see a baby.

And not just any baby, that baby is Emmanuel.

God with us.

In the middle of the mess, He is there.

In the middle of your mess, He is there.

If you want to rest merry today, you won't be able to if you look for joy and peace in your circumstances. You won't find it in family, friends, good food, familiar music, or presents. You'll only find it by looking closer and seeing the baby who came to give you something you never thought possible.

Look closer.

Because sometimes, when you look in a place where you think God would never be, He is there. It's why He came. Yes, He brought joy and peace to the world on Christmas. But He can bring joy and peace to your world today, too.

Because Emmanuel is here.

For you.

Merry Christmas, my friend. May this day surprise you. May it delight you. May you find unexpected laughter and quiet reflection. May your day be exactly what it should be, no more or less.

Rest merry and remember: Emmanuel is here!

DECEMBER 26

Surprise!

You thought the book was over, didn't you?

After all, once the day is over, who thinks about Christmas anymore?

Maybe you're one of those families that tears it all down on the 26th, or maybe you're one of those families who keeps it all up through New Year's. Or maybe—maybe—you're one of those people who everyone drives by and sees a Christmas tree up in February and we sadly shake our head and wonder why they "just can't let go of Christmas."

Did you rest merry yesterday?

Did you find joy—and choose it anyway, when it seemed hard to find?

Did you find peace, even in the middle of the noise and cacophony?

If you did a little better than last year, good job.

If you still struggled, good job—you tried, and resting merry takes more work than making the perfect gingerbread men. All the preparation, the planning, baking, buying, wrapping, decorating—it all led to one incredible, hopefully joyous day yesterday.

The day is over and you're asking yourself: what happens next?

That's where Mary and Joseph found themselves the day after the shepherds visited and told them that angels had just freaked the heck out of them and told them to go visit the baby in the manger.

A little tired and perhaps having a hard time waking up after the big day, they looked at each other, at the crying and hungry baby, still in swaddling clothes, lying in a manger, and asked, "What next?"

They didn't know what was ahead.

They didn't know they'd spend a couple years in Bethlehem. They didn't know about the temple visit and the old people waiting just to see their baby. They had no idea astronomers from the East had started a long journey that would eventually lead right to them. They would never have guessed that Egypt was ahead, nor the return to Nazareth, the eventual death of Joseph. And there's absolutely no way they would have guessed what lay in store for that baby angels had told them about.

What they did know?

That God was near.

He didn't stop being Emmanuel the day after His birth. In fact, He was nearer than ever, crawling, toddling, and eventually walking alongside them through every step their lives would now take.

It's the same for you and I today.

You don't know what's coming next. You don't know what the next week or the next year will hold. But that doesn't change the fact that God is still near. He is as close as a prayer, a cry for help, or even a whispered moment of fear.

Jesus' birth may have been the best night ever, but it means nothing if it doesn't give you what He really promised: the best life ever. Christmas doesn't end on the 26th. He didn't come to be with us for just one day. He came to be with us the next day, and the day after, and the following week, and into the new year, and well, you get it.

Rest merry because Emmanuel is here.

God with us.

On Christmas.

Today.

And forever.

DECEMBER 27

In the days of clean up after Christmas, it's easy to get a little blue.

After all, the world up until Christmas is full of twinkling lights, wonderfully nostalgic music, delicious smells, and moments of togetherness with people you love. And then it's over.

The recycling has overwhelmed the garage, the tree that looked so beautiful with gifts placed around it now just looks a little sad, and you start wondering about the number of cookies you may have eaten over the last couple days of celebrating.

I get it.

In our house, we take the tree down on December 26th, and we change from continuous Christmas music to a more generic "New Year's & Winter Mix." The Santa and Frosty are removed from the front porch. On the day after Christmas, we move on to looking forward to the New Year and what it will bring.

It's not easy to do.

I grew up in a house that kept the tree up until New Year, so adjusting to my wife's preference was tough.

If you're having trouble letting go of the holiday, ease yourself into it.

If you're missing the music, do what I do. Make a playlist with songs about winter that never mention Christmas (there are plenty) and throw in every version of "Auld Lang Syne" or "What are You Doing New Year's Eve?" as well, and you'll get some holiday-tinged songs without having to be reminded that Christmas is over.

Another way to ease yourself into the goodbye to Christmas? Grab a blank book and start writing. Journal and reflect on what you loved and what memories you'll never forget. That's resting merry, too. (Plus, you'll appreciate it when you get to be old and can't remember exactly what happened each year. As I'm not old, I can only guess that this true. Ahem.)

Just take time to find some peace in the middle of everything, in that kind of quiet week between Christmas and New Year's to remind yourself of the joy you've experienced.

Then save it for later in the year when you're wondering where your peace and joy went.

Because Christmas doesn't end at 11:59 pm on December 25th. If you truly believe that Emmanuel has come, it's just beginning.

So, even as you put away the trappings and trimming for this Christmas, don't put away the peace and the joy. Hang on to it, savor it , and rest in it throughout the next year.

DECEMBER 28

While it's wonderful to look forward to Christmas and all it represents, when we hang "can't let go of Christmas," we miss something.

Christmas isn't about the day itself.

That would be like reading the first chapter of a book and liking it so much that we never read the rest. Or watching the first ten minutes of a movie and then looping it back to the beginning. (Or like when you're watching Netflix and it gets stuck buffering. You know what I'm talking about.)

If we did that, we'd never read about Percy Jackson getting to Camp Half-Blood.

We'd think Joyce from *Stranger Things* was clearly looney.

We'd never find out why Harry Potter had that scar.

We'd think Bilbo never left his hobbit-hole.

We would be convinced that that poor Steve Rogers never made it into the army.

We might think the main characters in *Star Wars* were C3PO and R2D2.

And we'd never get past the "Circle of Life" in *The Lion King*.

Christmas is an incredibly wonderful and beautiful thing.

But it's just the beginning of the story.

If we stay in Christmas because it makes us happy and has great memories, we miss the chance to discover what comes next. We'd never find out about the travelers from the East and an evil king. We'd never know about the trip to Jerusalem and the long conversations with the wisest teachers. And even that is just the second and third part of the story. There's so much more, so much beyond "Away in a Manger" and "O Holy Night."

Perhaps we need to view Christmas like the opening moments of the film version of *The Lord of the Rings: The Fellowship of the Ring,* when Galadriel explains all that came before and all that is leading up to what will happen next in a great and epic adventure. Without that introduction of what happened in the past, we'd never be ready for what was coming next.

Or, if you prefer, think of the beginning of *Raiders of the Lost Ark* when we first see Indy in the jungle looking for the idol and slowly making his way through the traps and chambers until he eyes that piece of gold—and ends up running from a giant boulder. That moment helps us understand so much about the character and what he will do that we gladly follow him on his quest for the Ark.

Christmas helps us know the hero, the main character, and understand what makes Him special. And, just like these opening scenes, we realize the lights have just come down, the page has just been turned, and the story has just begun.

So the next time you're feeling melancholy over the end of Christmas, try looking at it a different way. Because this story is far, far from over. And we haven't even got to the best part yet.

DECEMBER 29

There's a reason why clock imagery is so prevalent in New Year's decorations. As the year draws down, we are all too aware of the winding down of time and how fast it really goes by.

Another way to say that is *time matters*.

In the seconds it takes you to read this sentence, time you will never get back is gone. Whether we like it or not, time slips quickly through our fingertips and the moment you thought you had to spend has vanished into memory. Wrist-watch time doesn't pause and give you time to think about what to do with it. It simply moves the hands of the clock forward, ever forward, asking you,

"What are you going to do with me?"

The older I get, the more I've been relentlessly pursuing the fact that time matters.

The time I have spent on my phone.

The time I have spent watching television.

The time I have spent reading a book.

The time I have spent writing a sentence.

The time I have spent teaching or playing or driving or yelling or praying or worshiping.

Every single moment in time matters.

And while what I do with my time matters at my job, or with my friends, or with my dreams, nothing matters more than the time I have with my children. So, if you're a parent (or going to be some day), this is particularly for you.

Time is short. From birth to high school graduation is less than 1,000 weeks. As much as I'd like it to be longer, it won't be. I can't lengthen it. I can only strengthen it.

Every year we celebrate milestones and birthdays and take vacations. We've celebrated Thanksgiving and Christmas.

And soon New Year will begin.

Week after week will pass into memory.

And time will ask, "What have you done with me?"

Time matters.

You have a limited number of weeks with your kids.

And it may be even more limited than you realize.

The clock will keep ticking.

Time will move on.

And you will be tired.

And you won't have enough money.

And you'll want some "alone time."

And.

And.

And.

Time will move on.

And one day, they won't ask anymore.

They won't ask you to dance.

They won't ask you to snuggle.

They won't ask you to pray with them or play with them or read to them or watch a movie with them.

Because one day, they will be gone.

And you'll ask time, "What did I do with you?"

So find time. Make time.

And if you've struggled in the last year, resolve to spend more time resting merry with the people who matter to you most. Then give them what matters most.

Time.

DECEMBER 30

I realized a few years ago that I am a worrier.

I may not come across like one, especially in my writing or public persona. I'm a generally positive person, I have a lot of joy, and I find much pleasure in simple things.

But I worry far more than I need to.

I figure out of the 525,600 minutes I had allotted to me this year, I spent at least 50,000 of them worrying.

And here's the sad thing: 99.9% of what I worried about never happened.

Every bill was paid.

We took vacations.

We traveled the country.

Our lights stayed on.

Our mortgage was paid.

We had birthday parties and Christmas presents.

Maybe you can relate. Maybe you've already started worrying about what the next year will bring. If so, I want to remind you that peace and joy are not found in the middle of a worried heart or spirit.

Worry isn't godly.

Worry isn't a spiritual gift.

It's a soul-sucking piece of nasty that the enemy uses to keep us from truly appreciating all of God's blessings and providence in our lives.

Nothing is accomplished by it. No good comes of it. One of the verses I've had to lean on more than once in my many years of worrying is this, where Jesus really makes clear what worry does to us:

"Can all your worrying add a single moment to your life?" (Matthew 6:27, NLT)

Worrying won't add anything to your life—it will only subtract from it. It will take away your joy and peace. The very idea of worrying is the exact opposite of resting merry. So as we begin to wrap up the holiday, let's wrap up our worries and put them where they belong: in the waste bin, far removed from us.

Let this next year be the year where you and I fully embrace God's grace and live our lives choosing joy and peace, the way that God intended us to live.

Resting merry in the fact that Emmanuel will be with us then, just like He was this Christmas.

DECEMBER 31

The year is nearly at an end. So is our time together.

We've spent the last 31 days thinking about what it means to pause and reflect on who God is and the incredible thing He did at Christmas. I called it *resting merry*. Maybe you've excelled at, maybe you'll need to try again next year.

Wherever you are today, I encourage you to look at the New Year with the hope that you will be filled with peace and find joy.

You can do it, you know.

The song we typically sing today reminds us that we can.

"Auld Lang Syne" is the traditional New Year's Eve song. It plays as the ball drops in Times Square, and we typically sing it right before we send the kids into the front yard to bang on pots and pans.

It's an old Scottish poem by Robert Burns. And it means "old long since," or to put it in a way that makes more sense, "long long ago." It starts with a question about the past, rightly asking "Is it right that old times be forgotten?"

The answer is, no.

Look back at the last 31 days. Look back at the last 365. Look back at the last years of your life and ask yourself how you did.

Maybe you've got more to regret than you wish.

Maybe you had the best year ever.

Maybe your life is going great, or maybe you wish you could get a do over.

Here, on the last night of the year, and the traditional end of the Christmas season, I want to remind you of something fundamentally important.

When God came to earth on Christmas, it was a fundamental shift and change in the way we know and relate to Him. The Incarnation is God's way of saying, "I'm not done with you, no matter what has happened. I'm going to be here now and I'll be here tomorrow, and I'm not going anywhere. It's right there in my name: Emmanuel. God with you!"

Don't let "auld days be forgot."

Whether they were good or bad, God was there.

And He's reminding you, as the new year begins, He will keep being there.

No matter what you face, He will be there.

I know, you're worried that it's too much of a mess.

Just a reminder: Christmas is all about finding God in the middle of the mess. It's where He often does His best work. So rest merry in the next year. He will be your peace. He will give you joy.

Because that's what He does best.

"They were terrified, but the angel reassured them. "Don't be afraid!" he said." (Luke 2:9b-10a, NLT)

HINTS FOR RESTING MERRY

As you've probably guessed, I love this holiday more than anything. When I was in college, I was called "Kris Kringle" by some girls in my dorm because they got a little tired of the Christmas music. I love to wear Santa Claus hats once Thanksgiving is over.

I take great pride in creating a beautiful scene out of our Dickens Christmas Village every year. I love Christmas lights and try to wrap each branch of the tree individually. And due to my huge Christmas music collection, my kids jokingly call me the King of Jingaling.

As you read the book, you may need some help feeling "merry" at times. Here are a few tips from someone who loves Christmas (but doesn't love all the work it would take to make it "Pinterest perfect").

TEN ALBUMS YOU SHOULD LISTEN TO THIS CHRISTMAS

10. *Christmastime* by Michael W. Smith

9. *A Charlie Brown Christmas* by Vince Guaraldi Trio

8. *Christmas the Cowboy Way* by Riders in the Sky

7. *Christmas* by Kurt Bestor

6. *Narada Christmas Collection, Volume 2* by Various Artists

5. *Christmas Night* by The Cambridge Singers

4. *Winter Moon* by Mindy Gleason

3. *The Muppet Christmas Carol* Original Motion Picture Soundtrack

2. *Christmas* by The Singers Unlimited

1. *The Andy Williams Christmas Album* by Andy Williams

(All available on Apple Music)

THIRTEEN CHRISTMAS MOVIES TO ENJOY

13. *Mystery Science Theater 3000: Santa Claus Conquers the Martians* (1991)

   The best TV show of all time skewers a very weird story about Santa Claus on Mars.

12. *The Bishop's Wife* (1947)

   Cary Grant leads the cast as an angel helping a pastor find his faith again.

11. *Mystery Science Theater 3000: Santa Claus* (1993)

   The devil and Santa fight for the soul of Lupita one Christmas Eve. Truly horrible.

10. *Home Alone* (1990)

   A true holiday classic, and John Williams' score is one of his best.

9. *The Year Without a Santa Claus/Santa Claus is Comin' to Town (TV Specials)* (1974/1970)

   The two greatest Rankin-Bass stop-motion animated specials, with great songs.

8. *Scrooge!* (1970)

   Albert Finney stars in this musical version of *A Christmas Carol*, and it's spectacular.

7. *A Christmas Story* (1983)

   It's a wonderful story about a family, and a dad who really truly loves his son.

6. *National Lampoon's Christmas Vacation* (1989)

   A bit raunchy, but every family has experienced this at least once during the holidays.

5. *The Muppet Christmas Carol* (1992)

   A nearly-perfect adaptation with fantastic songs and Michael Caine as Scrooge.

4. *The Polar Express* (2004)

   A family tradition to watch with hot cocoa and matching jammies. Do you believe?

3. *The Santa Clause* (1994) & *The Santa Clause 2: The Mrs. Clause* (2002)

   Tim Allen is the best Santa ever. There, I said it.

2. *A Christmas Carol* (1984)

   George C. Scott shines in this spectacular adaptation of the book.

1. *It's a Wonderful Life* (1946)

   Should be required viewing for all of us, and Jimmy Stewart was never better.

15 RULES OUR FAMILY LIVES BY AT CHRISTMAS

1. Memories matter. Say no to as many things as possible so you can create them.
2. Find the best Christmas lights in your city and go see them.
3. Drink lots of hot chocolate.
4. We don't care how you feel about Santa Claus. The bell still rings for us.
5. If you have kids, start staying home with them on Christmas Day.
6. Go to a great Christmas Eve service. Avoid loud and noisy, find quiet and peaceful.
7. Sleepovers under the Christmas tree are always acceptable.
8. Live trees really do rule.
9. Mix white and colored lights on the Christmas tree to make it look magical.
10. You don't get to get your parents out of bed until at least 7 am.
11. Having an open house on Christmas is a great way to see family and friends.
12. Daddy will cry at some point because he loves Christmas so much.
13. Make a lot of cookies. Calories don't count at Christmas.
14. Don't make a big meal on Christmas Day. Make a spread you can munch on all day.
15. Nobody makes fun of mommy when she's watching Hallmark Channel.

GIFT GIVING MADE EASY

Forget giving kids lots of presents. We do five: "Something to wear. Something to read. Something to play with. Something they need." Plus an ornament we choose specifically for them based on their personality, something that happened during the year, or something they liked a lot that year. When they move out, they'll have plenty of ornaments for their tree. My mom still gives me an ornament every year, so I have over 40 ornaments to fill our tree with after the kids move out.

We also stopped telling our kids which presents were theirs. We choose one set of wrapping paper for each child, wrap it in that paper, and then leave their names off. We hide a scrap of their paper at the bottom of the stocking so they won't know until they are done with stockings which presents are theirs. It makes the surprise of Christmas last!

Open toys right away and get busy playing Don't worry about the mess. (Remember, God is found in the middle of the mess!

BOOKS TO READ AT CHRISTMAS

1. *A Christmas Carol. In Prose. Being a Ghost Story of Christmas* by Charles Dickens

2. *God Came Near* by Max Lucado

3. *The Sphinx at Dawn* by Madeline L'Engle

4. *Skipping Christmas* by John Grisham

5. *The Nutcracker* by E.T.A. Hoffman

6. *The Manger is Empty* by Walter Wangerin

7. *The Gift of the Magi* by O. Henry

8. *The Best Christmas Pageant Ever* by Barbara Robinson

9. *Hercule Poirot's Christmas* by Agatha Christie

10. *How the Grinch Stole Christmas* by Dr. Seuss

11. *The Animals' Christmas* by Richard Scarry

12. *Miracle on 34th Street* by Valentine Davis

13. *Christmas Stories* by Charles Dickens

14. *The Polar Express* by Chris Van Allsburg

15. *Jacob's Gift* by Max Lucado

16. *How Mrs. Claus Saved Christmas* by Jeff Guinn

17. *Stories Behind the Best-Loved Songs of Christmas* by Ace Collins

18. *Santa Calls* by William Joyce

19. *Cranberry Christmas* by Wendy & Harry Devlín

20. This One. (Good job!)

FUN FACTS ABOUT CHRISTMAS

I've collected this Christmas trivia over the course of a few years and used it as the pre-show for many of my Christmas productions. It's fun to discover something new about something most people know so much about anyway. Use these bits of trivia to surprise and amaze your friends this holiday season, or use it against that know-it-all family member (but do it nicely, because it *is* Christmas, after all).

- The celebration of Christ's birth on December 25th did not become part of tradition until 320 AD, more than 300 years after His birth.

- A Christmas film classic, *Miracle on 34th Street*, was actually released in the summer of 1947. It won Oscars for Best Support Actor, Screenplay, and Original Story and was nominated for Best Picture.

- Alabama was the first state to declare Christmas a legal holiday–in 1836. At this time, most people worked on Christmas Day, including Congress.

- George Fredrich Handel composed *The Messiah* in just 24 days. He began writing on August 22, 1741 and did not eat or sleep until it was finished.

- The first Christmas card was made in 1843 by English painter and illustrator John Calcott Horsley.

- According to most historians, the earliest example of decorating a fir tree for Christmas took place in the small country of Latvia in the year 1510.

- The most-loved of all carols, "Stille Nacht" (Silent Night), was written in 1818 by an Austrian priest named Joseph Mohr.

- Charles Dickens' *A Christmas Carol*, published a week before Christmas in 1834, was an instant best-seller and remains his most popular novel.

- Arthur Rankin and Jules Bass created more than 17 Christmas specials, including *Frosty the Snowman, Rudolph, the Red-Nosed Reindeer, The Year Without a Santa Claus*, and more obscure ones like *Nestor, the Long-Eared Christmas Donkey*.

- Clement C. Moore, writing a poem for his children, invented the modern idea of Santa Claus in 1823 with the publication of *A Visit from St. Nicholas*, now better known as *The Night Before Christmas*.

- American political cartoonist Thomas Nast was the first artist to picture St. Nicholas, in a magazine illustration in 1870.

- The Dutch version of St. Nicholas, Sint Klauss, was brought to America by the settlers of New Amersterdam. He became Americanized in the early 1900's as Santa Claus.

- The image of Santa Claus we are most familiar with today is the result of a series of ads for the Coca-Cola Company. Dutch-born artist Haddon Sundblom created the modern look of Santa Claus in 1931.

- Considered by many to be *the* classic Christmas special, *A Charlie Brown Christmas* has been shown every year since 1965.

- "The Christmas Song" was written in 1944 by Mel Tormé and Bob Wells in an attempt to cool off during a hot Los Angeles summer.

- In 1856, President Franklin Pierce became the first President to decorate a Christmas tree in the White House.

- Noel, Virginia, is just one of 50 towns named Noel in the United States.

- Rankin-Bass' classic animated version of *Rudolph the Red-Nosed Reindeer* debuted on December 6, 1964, as part of the General Electric Fantasy Hour.

- Egg nog was first consumed in America in 1607. Captain John Smith reportedly made the first batch at Jamestown.

- The first live nativity scene was created by St. Francis of Assisi in 1224.

- Felix Mendelssohn wrote the music that became the melody of "Hark! The Herald Angels Sing" for an 1840 concert celebrating the invention of the printing press.

- The word "Christmas" entered the English language around the year 1050 as the Old English phrase "Christes masse," meaning "festival of Christ."

- In 1882, one of Thomas Edison's employees, Edward Johnson, put the first electric lights on a Christmas tree–a string of 80 lights he designed himself.

- The first "American" Christmas carol, "'Twas in the Moon of Wintertime" (The Huron Carol), was written by a Jesuit priest named Jean de Brébeuf. He wrote the songs to help the Huron Indians understand the birth of Christ.

- The inventor of modern color printing, American printer Lewis Prang, also created the first American Christmas card in 1874.

- In 1851, Mark Carr hauled two sleds loaded with trees from the Catskills to the streets of New York and opened the first retail Christmas tree lot in the United States.

- President Calvin Coolidge began the tradition of decorating a tree outside the White House in 1923.

- Ralph Blaine and Hugh Martin wrote the song "Have Yourself a Merry Little Christmas" for the film *Meet Me in St. Louis* in 1944. Its original context is one of sadness, as it is sung to comfort a little girl broken-hearted over her family's impending move. That's why the song suggests she "have a merry little Christmas now."

- There are eleven towns named Santa Claus in the United States.

- The original 1942 recording of "White Christmas" by Bing Crosby is the best-selling Christmas song of all time (and the best-selling single recording, too). It has sold more than 50 million copies.

- Russian tradition doesn't include Santa Claus. On January 1st, Grandfather Frost brings gifts to children.

- One of the most-loved films of all time, Frank Capra's *It's a Wonderful Life*, was released in 1946. It was a box-office disaster when it was first released and almost ruined the career of star Jimmy Stewart.

- The first Christmas postage stamp was issued in Canada in 1898. The United States didn't get around to making Christmas stamps until 1962.

- The best-selling Christmas album of all time remains Elvis Presley's *Elvis' Christmas Album*. It has sold over 10 million copies since it was released in 1957.

- The holidays have inspired countless classic films. It also inspired one of the worst movies ever made: *Santa Claus Conquers the Martians*, released in 1964.

- *Rudolph, the Red-Nosed Reindeer* did not start off as a song, but as a Montgomery Ward promotional book giveaway by staff copywriter Robert May.

- Poinsettias were brought to the United States from Mexico in 1828 by the first US Ambassador to Mexico, Joel Roberts Poinsett, for whom the plant was named.

There's a few fun facts to wow the family with when the conversation gets awkward this Christmas. You never know when one of those moments will happen, so keep these handy and maybe you'll turn this into one of those Christmases nobody wants to forget!

AFTERWORD

Through 20 years of ministry, my favorite season as a pastor was Christmas, because I got to remind families of this incredible, wonderful truth: the story of Christmas is the story of God coming near, of heaven coming to earth, of divinity wrapping itself in fragile humanity. Whether it was a Christmas production, a family event, a school play, a blog post, or a message during Advent, there's nothing better than reminding people of this amazing truth:

He was born on the BEST NIGHT EVER to give you the BEST LIFE EVER.

Rest merry, dear friend.

God is near.

ABOUT THE AUTHOR

DUANE S. MONTAGUE
has been writing about Christmas for a long time.
Whether it was creating stage musicals or a family outreach event,
a school play or an Advent message,
he's helped people see and experience the wonderful truth of Christmas for 20 years.
He has worked for the Walt Disney Company, Microsoft,
and two of the largest churches in the Pacific Northwest.
He is currently the Chief Storyteller at Thinks, LLC,
a company that helps people and businesses across the United States tell their stories.

He has been married to Robyn for 20 years.
They have four awesome kids and travel to
Disneyland and America's National Parks as often as possible.

He really really loves Christmas.

You can find more of his writings and works online at
duanesm.com & thinksinc.org

On social media, find him on
Twitter @dsmontague
Instagram @dsmontague
Facebook: dsmontague

Find more about *Resting Merry* on Facebook: restingmerry.

Made in the USA
San Bernardino, CA
28 December 2018